Tiny Talks

Volume 2—The Savior

A year's worth of simple messages that can be given during Primary or Family Home Evening

Tiny Talks

Volume 2—The Savior

A year's worth of simple messages that can be given during Primary or Family Home Evening

By Tammy & Chad Daybell

CFI

Springville, Utah

ISBN: 1-55517-617-8
v.1

Published by CFI
Imprint of Cedar Fort Inc.
www.cedarfort.com

Distributed by:

Cover design by Adam Ford
Cover design © 2002 by Lyle Mortimer
Illustrations © 2002 by Tammy Daybell

Printed in the United States of America
10 9 8 7 6 5 4 3 2 1

Printed on acid-free paper

Table of Contents

Introduction

We hope you found Volume 1 of this series to be helpful, and we hope this volume on the Savior will help your children learn more about his life and mission.

One new aspect of this volume is that since this is a chronological look at the Savior's life, two or more messages can be combined to create a longer talk.

As parents, we have experienced the challenge of writing Primary talks that are simple enough for our children to read, but that are interesting to the children in the audience. If you've faced the same difficulties, we truly hope these books are beneficial to you.

These talks can be used in many ways. If a talk is used in Primary, we suggest the child give the talk while holding up the picture at the appropriate time. The child could conclude with a short testimony about the topic, and close by saying, "In the name of Jesus Christ, amen."

We have found that visual aids greatly enhance a talk. With each talk we have listed pictures that could be used from the Gospel Art Picture Kit (GAPK). It is available from the Church Distribution Center. If you don't have one, your meetinghouse library might have a set. The meetinghouse library may also have other pictures available that fit the talk.

Tammy and Chad Daybell

Stories about Jesus in Tiny Talks: Volume 1

Several of the messages in *Tiny Talks Volume 1: Temples* are about the Savior. They are listed below, along with where to find them in Volume 1. Here in Volume 2 we purposely focus on other aspects of these stories, rather than repeat the same material.

Chapter 1

Jesus is our Savior

Jesus helped Heavenly Father create the earth

Scripture:

And worlds without number have I created; and I also created them for mine own purpose, and by the Son I created them, which is mine Only Begotten.
(Moses 1:33)

Jesus Christ is our wonderful friend. He loves us very much. He is also one of Heavenly Father's spirit children, and is our spirit brother. During pre-earth life, Jesus was the most obedient and righteous of all the spirit children. In a special meeting in heaven before we were born, Heavenly Father told us about his wonderful plan to make an earth. He told us we could receive bodies and be tested to see if we would obey the commandments.

Jesus was chosen to help create the earth. By using the power of the priesthood, he made the waters and the land, and placed all the plants and animals on the earth. When the earth was ready, Adam and Eve were placed in the Garden of Eden. Now it is our turn on earth to show Heavenly Father and Jesus that we will follow the plan. If we do, we will be able to live with them forever.

Visual Aids:
GAPK #100
The Creation
GAPK #240
Jesus The Christ

2

Jesus was chosen to save us from our sins

Before the earth was formed, we all attended a special meeting in heaven where Heavenly Father told us about the Plan of Salvation. We were very excited, because we learned we would be able to go to earth. We would be able to choose between good and evil.

If we lived righteously, we could become like Heavenly Father. But the plan required that someone be a Savior for us. Jesus said he would be our Savior and follow Heavenly Father's plan.

Another spirit known as Satan wanted us to follow a different plan. Satan wanted to force us to do good. We wouldn't have a choice. This would ruin the plan, so Heavenly Father chose Jesus to be the Savior. Satan became angry. He rebelled and was cast out of heaven.

When Jesus was on the earth, he paid the price for our sins by dying on the cross. We should always be grateful to the Savior for following Heavenly Father's plan.

Scripture:

Behold my Beloved son, which was my Beloved and Chosen from the beginning, said unto me — Father, thy will be done, and the glory be thine forever.
(Moses 4:2)

Visual Aid:
GAPK #230
The Crucifixion

Jesus visited many ancient prophets

Scripture:

And he saw the Lord, and he walked with him, and was before his face continually.
(D&C 107:49)

Visual Aid:
GAPK #120
Enoch and his people

When the earth was first created, Adam and Eve were placed in the Garden of Eden. They had a veil placed over their minds so they couldn't remember their pre-earth life. Heavenly Father and Jesus visited Adam and Eve in the garden to teach them the gospel.

Later, Jesus also visited other special prophets. The prophet Enoch lived before Noah's Flood, and he built a wonderful city. He built a temple, and Jesus would visit Enoch there. The scriptures say Enoch walked and talked with the Savior and learned many special things from him. Many years later, Jesus visited Moses and gave him the Ten Commandments.

The Prophet Joseph Smith also received many visits from Jesus. That is how the Savior tells his people what to do. Jesus talks to his prophet, and the prophet then tells us the messages Jesus wants us to hear. Jesus loves each of us very much, and he wants us to follow the commandments so we can return and live with him.

4

The brother of Jared saw Jesus as a spirit

Long ago the Lord guided a group of righteous people called the Jaredites toward the Promised Land. He told them to build boats like submarines so they could cross the ocean. They were led by two righteous men, Jared, and his brother. They were worried about how they would see inside these boats. Finally the brother of Jared decided to carve out sixteen stones and ask Jesus to light them.

Jesus told him it was a good plan and touched each stone with his finger. When he touched the stones, the brother of Jared saw the Savior's finger! He told Jesus what he had seen, and Jesus was happy, because it meant the brother of Jared had great faith. Jesus then showed him his whole spirit body. Jesus hadn't been born yet, but he looked like a full-grown man. Jesus explained that our body is just a covering for our spirit.

Scripture:

Behold, this body, which ye now behold, is the body of my spirit; and man have I created after the body of my spirit; and even as I appear unto thee to be in the spirit will I appear unto my people in the flesh.
(Ether 3:16)

Visual Aid:
GAPK #318
The Brother of Jared Sees the Finger of the Lord

Chapter 2

Jesus came to a special family

Mary was chosen to be the mother of Jesus

Scripture:

He raised up unto them David to be their king ... and said, I have found David the son of Jesse, a man after mine own heart, which shall fulfill all my will. Of this man's seed hath God according to his promise raised unto Israel a Savior, Jesus.
(Acts 13:22-23)

Visual Aid:
GAPK #201
The Nativity

Jesus was born to a special person. Her name was Mary. She was specially chosen by Heavenly Father to be the mother of Jesus. She grew up near the city of Jerusalem. One of her ancestors was King David, who killed the giant Goliath in battle. Heavenly Father had told his prophets the Savior would be a descendant of David, so this fulfilled an important prophecy.

Jesus is the Only Begotten Son of God, meaning Heavenly Father is his father. But since Heavenly Father doesn't live on earth, a righteous man named Joseph was chosen to be Mary's husband and help raise Jesus. Joseph was a carpenter, and he taught Jesus to work hard and do what is right.

Mary and Joseph knew what a special son Jesus was. They watched over him and protected him, because they knew that someday he would become the Savior of the World.

The angel Gabriel visited Mary

When Mary was a young woman she received a special visit from an angel named Gabriel. She was a little afraid of the heavenly messenger, because he was surrounded by a glorious light. But the angel told her not to worry. He said she had been chosen for a special mission in life and was blessed above all other women. She would be the mother of Jesus Christ, the Son of God.

Mary was nervous, but the angel explained that the Holy Ghost would come upon her and everything would be all right. He also told her that her cousin Elisabeth would also have a son. Mary was surprised, because Elisabeth was much older than she was and no one thought she would ever have children. But a miracle had happened, and Elisabeth's son would grow up to be a very important prophet named John the Baptist. He would prepare the way for Jesus, and be the one to baptize the Savior.

Scripture:

And the angel said unto her, Fear not, Mary: for thou hast found favour with God. And behold, thou shalt conceive in thy womb, and bring forth a son, and shalt call his name Jesus. He shall be great, and shall be called the Son of the Highest. (Luke 1:30-32)

Visual Aid:
GAPK # 241
The Annunciation: The Angel Gabriel Appears to Mary

Mary goes to visit her cousin Elisabeth

Scripture:

And Mary arose in those days, and went into the hill country ... and entered into the house of Zacharius, and saluted Elisabeth. And it came to pass that when Elisabeth heard the saluta- tion of Mary, the babe leaped in her womb; and Elisabeth was filled with the Holy Ghost. And she spake out with a loud voice, and said, Blessed art thou among women.
(Luke 1:39-42)

Visual Aid:
GAPK #208
John the Baptist Baptizing
Jesus

After the angel Gabriel visited Mary to tell her she would be the mother of Jesus, she didn't share this secret with anyone. She didn't tell her parents, or even her future husband Joseph. Finally she decided to visit her cousin Elisabeth in another city. The angel had told Mary that Elisabeth was also going to have a son. Elisabeth's son would grow up to be John the Baptist and someday baptize Jesus. Mary hoped Elisabeth would understand how she was feeling.

When Mary arrived at Elisabeth's house, a very interesting thing happened. The baby boy in Elisabeth's belly jumped as if he were very happy! Then the Holy Ghost let Elisabeth know about Mary's special calling as the mother of Jesus. Elisabeth told Mary, "Blessed art thou among women."

So Mary was able to share her secret with Elisabeth. Mary stayed there for three months until John the Baptist was born, then she returned to her family.

10

Joseph learns he will be Mary's husband

Heavenly Father knew Jesus would need a special, righteous father while he grew up. He chose Joseph to be that person.

Joseph and Mary were planning to be married, but Joseph was worried when he found out Mary was going to have a baby. He wondered if he should still marry her. But the angel Gabriel visited Joseph in a dream. The angel told Joseph that even though Mary was already pregnant, he should marry her.

The angel told Joseph that the baby in Mary's belly was the Son of God and would be the Savior. The angel also told Joseph that the baby should be named Jesus, just as all the prophets had said his name would be.

After the angel's visit, Joseph and Mary were soon married, and they made a home in the town of Nazareth. They waited excitedly for Jesus to be born.

Scripture:

Behold, the angel of the Lord appeared unto him in a dream, saying, Joseph ... fear not to take unto thee Mary thy wife: for that which is conceived in her is of the Holy Ghost. And she shall bring forth a son, and thou shalt call his name Jesus, for he shall save his people from their sins.
(Matthew 1:20-21)

Visual Aid:
GAPK #201
The Nativity

Chapter 3

The birth of Jesus

Scripture:

And she brought forth her firstborn son, and wrapped him in swaddling clothes, and laid him in a manger; because there was no room for them in the inn.
(Luke 2:7)

Visual Aid:
GAPK #200
The Birth of Jesus

Jesus was born in an unusual place. When Mary was nearly ready to give birth to Jesus, the emperor told the people they had to return to the home of their ancestors to be counted and taxed. This meant Mary and Joseph had to travel to Bethlehem, also known as the City of David, their famous ancestor. Bethlehem was many miles away from their home, so Joseph placed Mary upon a donkey, and they made a long, slow journey on dusty roads. When they arrived at Bethlehem, the city was filled with many other visitors. Joseph tried to find a place for them to stay, but there weren't any rooms available.

Joseph was getting very worried, but finally one of the inn owners said Mary and Joseph could stay in his stable, where animals such as cows and donkeys were kept. Joseph did his best to make Mary comfortable. Later that night, Jesus was born. They wrapped him in swaddling clothes and tenderly placed him in the soft hay of the manger. Very few people in the city knew this special baby had been born, but everyone in heaven was very happy, because the Savior of the World was born.

Shepherds come to visit the newborn king

On the night that Jesus was born in a stable in Bethlehem, there were shepherds in the nearby fields watching their sheep. They were in for a big surprise. Suddenly the dark night turned bright as day and an angel appeared to them. He told them not to be afraid, and that he had an important message for them. He told them the Savior of the World had been born that night in their city, and he invited them to visit this special child. He told them they would find him wrapped in swaddling clothes, lying in a manger.

After the angel left, the shepherds quickly went down into Bethlehem to find the newborn king. They were able to find the stable, and they looked on in amazement at the little baby sleeping in the hay. They knew he was the Son of God. After visiting Jesus, they ran to tell their friends and family that they had seen the Savior. Then they returned to their sheep, giving thanks to Heavenly Father for letting them see Jesus.

Scripture:

And there were in the same country shepherds abiding in the field, keeping watch over their flock by night . . . And the angel said unto them, Fear not: for behold, I bring you good tidings of great joy, which shall be to all people. For unto you is born this day in the City of David a Saviour, which is Christ the Lord.
(Luke 2:8-11)

Visual Aid:
GAPK #202
The Announcement of Christ's Birth to the Shepherds

The Nephites have a night without darkness

When Jesus was born in Bethlehem, Heavenly Father gave his children living on the other side of the world a special sign. At the time of the Savior's birth, the sun was just going down in the Americas. Then an amazing thing happened. The sun went down, but it was still as light as day. There wasn't any darkness all night. Then the sun came up again, right on schedule.

This was a great day for the righteous Nephites, because the wicked Nephites had planned to kill them if the sign didn't come that night. But it did, and the wicked Nephites fell to the ground in fear. This great sign fulfilled the prophecy Samuel the Lamanite had made to the Nephites. Five years earlier Samuel had said that when the Savior was born, there would be a night without darkness.

The next night was also special. When the sun went down again, the people could see the beautiful new star in the sky that was also a sign that Jesus was born.

16

Baby Jesus is taken to the priest

When Jesus was eight days old, Mary and Joseph took him to a priest to receive his name, similar to when we give babies a name and a blessing in Sacrament Meeting. He was given the name of Jesus, just as the angel Gabriel had told Mary and Joseph to do. A month later, Jesus was taken by his parents to the temple in Jerusalem, where he was dedicated to the Lord.

When a baby was taken to the temple, the parents were expected to buy a lamb to be sacrificed in remembrance of the Lord. If the family didn't have enough money to buy a lamb, they could sacrifice two doves. Since Mary and Joseph were poor, they bought two doves.

While they were at the temple, two people were told by the Holy Ghost that the Savior was there. One was named Simeon, who had waited his whole life to see the Savior. The other person was Anna, a great follower of Heavenly Father. She saw the Baby Jesus and said he would someday redeem mankind from their sins.

Scripture:

His name was called Jesus, which was so named of the angel. ... They brought him to Jerusalem, to present him to the Lord ... and to offer a sacrifice according to that which is said in the law of the Lord, a pair of turtledoves, or two young pigeons.
(Luke 2:22-24)

Visual Aid:
GAPK #118
Temple Used Anciently

Chapter 4

The childhood of Jesus

The Wise Men travel to see Jesus

Scripture:

And lo, the star, which they saw in the east, went before them, till it came and stood over where the young child was. When they saw the star, they rejoiced with exceeding great joy. And when they were come into the house, they saw the young child with Mary his mother, and fell down, and worshipped him: and when they had opened their treasures, they presented unto him gifts; gold, and frankincense, and myrrh.
(Matthew 2:9-11)

Visual Aid:
GAPK #203
The Wise Men

When Jesus was born in Bethlehem, the Wise Men were still very far away. They lived in a country far to the East, but on the night Jesus was born, they saw a beautiful new star in the sky. They knew this was the sign that the Savior had been born.

Their journey to Jerusalem took many weeks. When they arrived, they expected the people of Jerusalem to be very excited the Savior had been born. But no one seemed to know about Jesus. When they traveled toward Bethlehem, the new star appeared again in the heavens, and guided them to the Savior's home in Bethlehem.

When they finally arrived, the Wise Men saw Jesus and fell to their knees. They were so happy to see him. They gave the family many expensive treasures and gifts. Mary and Joseph were very happy to have such wonderful visitors.

Joseph takes his family to Egypt

King Herod ruled Jerusalem when Jesus was born. Herod was a wicked man who had killed many people. He heard a baby had been born who would become the King of the Jews. He was angry and wanted to kill the baby before he could grow up and become a leader. So King Herod ordered his men to kill all the children in Bethlehem under the age of two.

Heavenly Father knew what King Herod had ordered, and he sent an angel to visit Joseph in a dream. The angel told Joseph that Jesus' life was in danger, and that he should take Mary and Jesus far away to the country of Egypt. They would be safe there.

So Joseph quickly packed their belongings and took his family to Egypt, where they stayed until King Herod died a few years later. After the king's death, an angel visited Joseph in Egypt and told him it was safe to return home. Mary and Joseph chose to live in the city of Nazareth, where Jesus would grow up.

Scripture:

Behold, the angel of the Lord appeared to Joseph in a dream, saying, Arise, and take the young child and his mother, and flee into Egypt, and be thou there until I bring thee word: for Herod will seek the young child to destroy him. When he arose, he took the young child and his mother by night, and departed into Egypt: And was there until the death of Herod.
(Matthew 2:13-15)

Visual Aid:
GAPK #204
Flight Into Egypt

Heavenly Father blessed young Jesus

Scripture:

And the child grew, and waxed strong in spirit, filled with wisdom: and the grace of God was upon him.
(Luke 2:40)

The scriptures don't say very much about Jesus' daily life as a young boy, but the prophets have told us he spent much time learning the gospel. Jesus also discovered he was the Son of God. In the New Testament we learn that Jesus was filled with wisdom, and Heavenly Father was watching over him. Mary and Joseph also kept a close watch on Jesus.

Jesus had a special mission to fulfill, but he also lived a normal life. As a Jewish boy, he attended school and studied the scriptures. He learned two languages—Hebrew and Aramaic. He also knew many Greek and Latin words. When he was twelve years old, his family traveled to Jerusalem for a feast. Afterward, his family couldn't find him. He was at the temple, talking to men about the gospel and answering their questions.

We know that Jesus lived a sinless life. He may have gotten angry or disappointed at times, as we all do, but he kept all of Heavenly Father's commandments.

Visual Aid:
GAPK #205
Boy Jesus in the Temple

Jesus had many brothers and sisters

From the scriptures we learn that Jesus wasn't the only child of Mary and Joseph. Jesus was the oldest child, but he had at least four brothers and two sisters. So it was a rather large family. Being in such a family helped Jesus learn patience, kindness, and how to get along with other people. As a Jewish family, they spent much time together in prayer and scripture study.

Joseph was a carpenter, and he taught Jesus how to work with wood and build houses and furniture. As Jesus grew up, he wasn't well-known outside of his town. He probably just had a few friends like we do.

The Jewish custom was that a man could not become a minister until he was thirty years old, so Jesus waited patiently for that day to arrive. Sometime before Jesus turned thirty, Joseph died. After Joseph's death, Jesus most likely spent much of his time helping his mother and taking care of the carpentry shop, waiting until he could preach the gospel.

Scripture:

Is not this the carpenter, the son of Mary, the brother of James, and Joses, and of Juda, and Simon? And are not his sisters here with us?
(Mark 6:3)

Visual Aid:
GAPK #206
Childhood of Jesus Christ

Chapter 5

Jesus prepares to preach the gospel

Jesus started preaching the gospel at age 30

Scripture:

And Jesus increased in wisdom and stature, and in favor with God and man.
(Luke 2:52)

Jesus grew up to become a strong, wonderful man. When Jesus learned that he would be the Savior of the World, he still wasn't old enough to start preaching the gospel. When Jesus lived on earth, there was a tradition in Jerusalem that a man could not become a minister until the age of 30.

As Jesus approached that age, he realized he would have to leave his family. He would no longer work as a carpenter. Heavenly Father had a special mission for him to perform.

The Savior knew his calling in life was to preach the gospel to the people, and then pay the price for our sins. Jesus was eager to begin his ministry.

He knew his cousin John the Baptist had started teaching the people, telling them to repent and be baptized. John's teachings prepared the way for the people to accept Jesus as the Savior.

Visual Aid:
GAPK #207
John Preaching in the Wilderness

Jesus is baptized by John the Baptist

A few months before Jesus began his ministry, his cousin John the Baptist began teaching the people. John told the people about the Savior, and that he would be coming soon. He taught the people to repent and be baptized to wash away their sins. He taught them that Jesus would come and give them the gift of the Holy Ghost.

One day Jesus went to the Jordan River, where John was baptizing people. Jesus asked John to baptize him, but John knew the Savior was sinless, and did not need to be baptized. But Jesus explained that Heavenly Father had commanded all people to be baptized. So they went down into the water. John said the baptismal prayer and put Jesus all the way under the water. When Jesus came out of the water, Heavenly Father's voice could be heard saying, "This is my beloved Son, in whom I am well pleased." Then John the Baptist saw the Holy Ghost descend like a dove out of heaven and rest upon Jesus. That was a very special day in the Savior's life.

Scripture:

And it came to pass in those days, that Jesus came from Nazareth of Galilee, and was baptized of John in Jordan. And straightway coming up out of the water, he saw the heavens opened, and the Spirit like a dove descending upon him: And there came a voice from heaven, saying, Thou art my beloved Son, in whom I am well pleased. (Mark 1:9-11)

Visual Aid:
GAPK #208
John the Baptist Baptizing Jesus

27

Jesus fasts forty days, then Satan tempts him

Scripture:

And he was there in the wilderness forty days, tempted of Satan; and was with the wild beasts; and the angels ministered unto him.
(Mark 1:13)

Visual Aid:
GAPK #240
Jesus the Christ

After his baptism, Jesus went into the wilderness to learn from Heavenly Father the things he should do to become our Savior. Jesus spent forty days there alone, except for visits from angels. He fasted the whole time, meaning he didn't have anything to eat or drink.

When the forty days were over, Satan came to tempt Jesus. Satan knew Jesus held the priesthood and could do miracles. Satan also knew Jesus hadn't eaten anything for forty days. Satan told Jesus to change rocks into bread. But Jesus told him no, because he knew that wasn't the right way to use his priesthood power. Next, Jesus went to the top of temple. Satan came again. He told Jesus to jump off the temple to see if Heavenly Father would save him. Satan said angels would catch Jesus before he hit the ground. But Jesus said he wouldn't jump.

Then Jesus went to the top of a mountain. Jesus was shown all the riches and kingdoms of the world. Satan told Jesus he could have all the money in the world if he would follow Satan. Jesus said no. He commanded Satan to leave him alone, and Satan left. Jesus had passed his test.

Jesus chooses his apostles

Soon after Jesus began teaching the people he knew he needed to choose men who could be leaders in his church. Jesus knew a man who lived nearby named Peter who had been chosen by Heavenly Father to help start the church. Peter was a fishermen who would go in his boat onto the Sea of Galilee and use big nets to catch fish. He would sell the fish to people in his town.

One day Peter and his friends returned from fishing all night. They hadn't caught any fish and were very unhappy. Jesus was on the shore, and told Peter to try one more time. Peter obeyed Jesus, and this time Peter caught so many fish in his nets that it filled his boat and another boat, too! Peter and his friends, James and John, knew Jesus had made a miracle happen.

When they came to the shore, Jesus told the men to leave their boats and follow him. They obeyed, and soon Jesus called Peter, James and John to be apostles in his church. Jesus also chose nine other men as apostles. Jesus ordained them to the priesthood, and they started teaching the gospel.

Scripture:

And when it was day, he called unto him his disciples, and of them he chose twelve, whom also he named apostles; Simon (whom he also named Peter,) and Andrew his brother, James and John, Philip and Bartholomew, Matthew and Thomas, James the son of Alpheus, and Simon called Zelotes, and Judas the brother of James, and Judas Iscariot. (Luke 6:13-16)

Visual Aids:
GAPK #209
Calling of the Fisherman
GAPK #211
Christ Ordaining the Apostles

Chapter 6

Jesus begins his ministry

Jesus is rejected by the people in Nazareth

Scripture:

*And all they in the syna-
gogue, when they heard
these things, were filled
with wrath, and rose up,
and thrust him out of the
city, and led him unto the
brow of the hill whereon
their city was built, that
they might cast him down
headlong, but he passing
through the midst of them
went his way.*
(Luke 4:28-30)

Visual Aid:
GAPK #240
Jesus the Christ

After Jesus began his ministry, he decided to visit Nazareth, the city where he grew up. He wanted his friends and neighbors to know who he truly was. Jesus went to their church and read prophecies to the people about the Savior from the scriptures. Then he closed the scriptures and told them the verses he had read were about him.

His friends and neighbors didn't believe he was the Son of God. They had known him for many years and only knew him as Joseph and Mary's son. The people wanted him to show them a miracle to prove he was the Savior, but Jesus told them he would not do miracles for people who didn't have faith. The people were angry and took him to the top of a hill. They wanted to throw him off the edge of a cliff. But Jesus used his priesthood power to escape from the group before they could hurt him. So it turned out the people of Nazareth did witness a miracle—just not one they had expected.

Jesus blesses the children

Jesus loves little children, because they have the wonderful qualities of faith, kindness, happiness, love and trust. When Jesus was teaching his apostles, he told them they should also have these qualities.

One time there was a big crowd around Jesus, including many children who wanted to meet him. The apostles thought Jesus was too busy to talk with the children, and told their parents to take them away. But Jesus heard them, and he was sad that his apostles had turned the children away. Even though he was busy, he told the apostles to bring the little children to him. He took the children in his arms, talked with them, and gave each of them a special blessing.

Later, when Jesus visited the Nephites after his resurrection, he also took special care to bless all the children. Little children are very precious to him.

Scripture:

Verily I say unto you, Whosoever shall not receive the kingdom of God as a little child, he shall not enter therein. And he took them up in his arms, put his hands upon them, and blessed them. (Mark 10:15-16)

Visual Aid:
GAPK #216
Christ and the Children

Jesus teaches Nicodemus about baptism

Scripture:

Nicodemus, a ruler of the Jews, ... came to Jesus by night, and said unto him, Rabbi, we know that thou art a teacher come from God: for no man can do these miracles that thou doest, except God be with him. . . . Jesus answered and said unto him, Verily, verily, I say unto thee, Except a man be born of water and the spirit, he cannot enter into the kingdom of God. (John 3:1-5)

Visual Aids:
GAPK #208 John the Baptist Baptizing Jesus
GAPK #602
The Gift of the Holy Ghost

The religious leaders of Jerusalem didn't like Jesus. They were wicked men who were afraid the people would make Jesus the king. But one of these men had a good heart. His name was Nicodemus. One night he found Jesus and told him he believed the miracles he had seen Jesus do. He asked Jesus to teach him.

Jesus knew Nicodemus needed to learn the first principles and ordinances of the gospel. Jesus told him that a person needed to be born of the water and of the spirit, meaning to be baptized and to receive the Holy Ghost. Nicodemus became a friend of Jesus, but he decided not to join the church.

It is important that when people believe the gospel and want to follow Jesus, they must be baptized and become members of the true church. Then, if they obey the commandments, they can live someday in the Celestial Kingdom with him.

The Sermon on the Mount

One day Jesus climbed a mountain near the Sea of Galilee. Many people followed him. They wanted to hear the gospel and learn how to live again with Heavenly Father. Jesus taught them a special message that is now known as the Sermon on the Mount.

Jesus told the people how they could be happy. He said we should do our best to keep the commandments, and to tell the truth. Jesus said the most important thing is to love other people. He taught that we should forgive other people, even if they are mean to us. Jesus said Heavenly Father would bless those who are kind to others and are peacemakers.

Jesus said we shouldn't be afraid of sharing the gospel with other people. He said we should be like a light on a hill that everyone can see. He meant we should live so everyone knows we want to obey Heavenly Father, and they can follow our example. If we follow the teachings Jesus gave during the Sermon on the Mount, we will be happy and live again with Heavenly Father.

Scripture:

And seeing the multitudes, he went up into a mountain; and when he was set, his disciples came unto him. And he opened his mouth and taught them. (Matthew 5:1-2)

Visual Aid:
GAPK #212
The Sermon on the Mount

Chapter 7

Jesus travels among the people

Jesus performed many miracles

Scripture:

Now when the sun was setting, all they that had any sick with divers diseases brought them unto him; and he laid his hands on every one of them, and healed them.
(Luke 4:40)

Heavenly Father gave Jesus the priesthood, which is the power of God. With that power, Jesus was able to perform many miracles among the people. Some of these people were born blind, but Jesus blessed them and made them see. He also healed people who could not walk, hear or talk, or had injured bodies. These people were grateful to Jesus for making them well.

One time Jesus was traveling on a boat with his apostles. Jesus fell asleep, and soon the wind began to blow very hard. Big waves crashed against the boat. The apostles were afraid, and they worried the boat would sink. They woke up Jesus and asked him to help them. Jesus went to the front of the boat and used his priesthood power to command the wind and waves to stop. The weather changed instantly, and the boat was safe. The apostles were amazed that the wind and waves had obeyed him. Jesus told them to have more faith and use their priesthood. Then they could also perform miracles.

Visual Aid:
GAPK #214
Stilling the Storm

The importance of the Sabbath day

The wicked leaders in Jerusalem made very strict rules about what people could do on the Sabbath day. Many of the rules didn't make sense. But Jesus knew the Sabbath is a day people are supposed to do good things and help each other, so he would often heal people who were blind and deaf on the Sabbath day.

One Sabbath day the wicked leaders followed Jesus into a church. Inside was a man who had a hurt hand. The leaders wanted to see if Jesus would heal the man. Jesus told the man to stretch forth his hand, and his hand was healed. Jesus wasn't afraid of the leaders. He did what was right.

We can do many good things on the Sabbath day to make it different from the other days of the week. We can attend church, write in our journals and study the scriptures. We can also visit sick people and help others feel better on this special day.

Scripture:

And he saith unto them, Is it lawful to do good on the Sabbath days, or to do evil? . . . He saith to the man, Stretch forth thine hand. And he stretched it out: and his hand was restored whole as the other.
(Mark 3:3,5)

Visual Aid:
GAPK #213
Jesus Healing the Blind

Only one leper thanked Jesus

Scripture:

And as he entered into a certain village, there met him ten men that were lepers, which stood afar off. And they lifted their voices and said, Jesus, Master, have mercy on us. And when he said unto them, Go show yourselves unto the priests. And it came to pass that, as they went, they were cleansed.
(Luke 17:12-14)

Visual Aid:
GAPK #221
The Ten Lepers

Leprosy was a disease that was common during Jesus' time. The disease caused sores all over a person's body, and sometimes the skin would even fall off. People with the disease were called lepers. The doctors did not know how to help them.

Jesus had the power to heal any illness, and one day ten lepers asked Jesus to heal them. Jesus told them to go meet with their priests. They did, and on the way their disease went away. They were healed because they had faith that Jesus could heal them.

Only one of the lepers returned to thank Jesus for healing him. Jesus asked him where the other nine men had gone. Jesus was happy the man was grateful. Heavenly Father and Jesus are happy when we show gratitude, and tell them in our prayers we are thankful for all our blessings.

Jesus raises Lazarus from the dead

One day a messenger brought Jesus terrible news. His good friend Lazarus was very sick in a distant town called Bethany. Jesus loved Lazarus and wanted to bless him. But by the time Jesus got to Bethany, Lazarus had been dead for four days. His family was very sad. They knew Jesus could have healed him if he had arrived before Lazarus died. But Jesus told the family that Lazarus would live again.

The family took Jesus to the tomb where Lazarus was buried. Jesus told them to move the stone from the opening of the tomb. Jesus called out, "Lazarus, come forth." When he said that, the spirit of Lazarus left the Spirit World and returned to his body. Lazarus then walked out of the tomb. Everyone was happy, especially his family. Jesus had performed a wonderful miracle.

Scripture:

And when he thus had spoken, he cried with a loud voice, Lazarus, come forth. And when he that was dead came forth, bound head and foot with grave clothes: and his face was bound about with a napkin. Jesus saith unto them, Loose him, and let him go.
(John 11:43-44)

Visual Aid:
GAPK #222
Jesus Raising Lazarus from the Dead

Chapter 8

Jesus teaches through stories

The talents

Jesus often taught the gospel by a telling a story. This made it easier for the people to understand the message. Jesus once told a story about a rich man who gave his servants some money to use. Then the man went on a long trip. When he came back, he asked the servants what they had done with the money he had given them. Some had used the money to make more money. But one had buried it in the ground and didn't use it at all. The rich man was angry, because the servant hadn't used what he had been given.

Jesus taught his apostles that each of us have been given special gifts by Heavenly Father. These are called talents. We are to use them while on earth to improve ourselves and help others. When we don't use our talents, Heavenly Father is sad. He wants us to use our talents to become better people and strengthen the church. If we are good and faithful servants, we will be very blessed.

Scripture:

His lord said unto him, Well done, thou good and faithful servant; thou has been faithful over a few things, I will make thee ruler over many things: enter thou into the joy of the lord.
(Matthew 25:23)

Visual Aid:
GAPK #211
Christ Ordaining the Apostles

The lost sheep

Jesus told the story of a shepherd that had 100 sheep. The shepherd took his sheep to the hills, and one of them got lost. The shepherd left the other sheep to go find the lost one. After much searching, he finally found the missing sheep. When he returned home, he called all his friends and neighbors to his house so they could celebrate finding the lost sheep.

Just like the sheep, every person on earth is important. Jesus is sad when one of us makes wrong choices and is lost. Jesus loves us very much and wants everyone to return and live with Heavenly Father. When we help someone do what is right, we are like the shepherd. Jesus is very happy when we help bring people back to church through our good example and friendship. We are all precious to the Savior.

Scripture:

What man of you, having an hundred sheep, if he lose one of them, doth not leave the ninety and nine in the wilderness, and go after that which is lost, until he find it? And when he hath found it, he layeth it on his shoulders, rejoicing.
(Luke 15:4-5)

Visual Aid:
GAPK #216
Christ and the Children

The Prodigal Son

Scripture:

And he arose, and came to his father. And when he was yet a great way off, his father saw him, and had compassion . . . And the son said, Father, I have sinned against heaven . . . But the father said to his servants . . . For this my son was dead, and is alive again; he was lost, and is found.
(Luke 15:20-24)

Visual Aid:
GAPK #220
The Prodigal Son

Jesus told the people about a young farm boy who wanted to go live in the city. He asked his father to give him some money. The father wasn't happy, but he gave his son a lot of money and let him go live in the city. The son made many bad choices. He didn't obey the commandments of God. He wasted all of his money. He didn't even have money to buy food. He finally found a job feeding pigs. He felt bad about the choices he had made. He wanted to go home, but he knew he had sinned. He decided to ask to be a servant in his father's house.

The son returned home. His father welcomed him with a hug and said he didn't have to be a servant. The son had lost many things, but the father was happy he decided to return home and repent. Heavenly Father feels the same way. If we do wrong, he still wants us to come back. If we make a bad choice, we can repent and return to him.

46

The Good Samaritan

One day a leader of the Jews asked Jesus how to get into heaven. Jesus told him to love his neighbor. The man asked, "Who is my neighbor?" So Jesus told him this story.

A man was walking along a road and was attacked by thieves. He was badly hurt. The first person to see him was a Jewish priest, but the priest didn't help him. Next came a Jewish man who worked in the temple. He didn't help the man, either. Then came a Samaritan man. The Jews thought they were better than the Samaritans. But this Samaritan stopped and helped the injured Jewish man. He even took him to town and cared for him. As Jesus ended the story, he asked the man, "Who was the man's neighbor?"

The Jewish leader knew the Samaritan had been the best neighbor, because he had helped the injured man. Jesus told the man to be like the Samaritan. Jesus wants us to be kind to everyone, too.

Scripture:

But a certain Samaritan, as he journeyed, came where he was; and when he saw him, he had compassion on him. And went to him, and bound up his wounds . . . and brought him to an inn, and took care of him.
(Luke 10:33-34)

Visual Aids:
GAPK #218
The Good Samaritan

Chapter 9

Jesus completes the Atonement

The Last Supper

Jesus taught the people for three years, but he knew the time was coming for him to pay the price for our sins. The Savior's sacrifice is called the Atonement, meaning he died for us, and will redeem us if we live righteously.

Jesus traveled to Jerusalem on a donkey for the Feast of the Passover. Large crowds welcomed him to the city. They knew Jesus could do miracles, and many believed he was the Son of God. Jesus went to a large room to eat with his apostles. Jesus knew this would be his last meal on earth. It is called the Last Supper.

During this supper Jesus taught the apostles about the Sacrament. He told them it would be a reminder that he would bleed and suffer to take away their sins. He told them he would die, but that three days later he would rise up again. We still take the Sacrament each week to remind us of everything that Jesus did for us. It is the main purpose of Sacrament Meeting.

Scripture:

And as they were eating, Jesus took bread, and blessed it, and brake it, and gave it to the disciples, and said, Take, eat; this is my body. And he took the cup, and gave thanks, and gave it to them, saying, Drink ye all of it; For this is my blood of the new testament, which is shed for many for the remission of sins.
(Matthew 26:26-28)

Visual Aids:
GAPK #223
Triumphal Entry
GAPK #225
The Last Supper

Jesus suffers in the Garden of Gethsemane

After eating the Last Supper, Jesus went to the Garden of Gethsemane to pray. Jesus knew he had been chosen to be the Savior of the World, and the time had come to pay the price for our sins. Jesus asked Heavenly Father to bless him, because he could feel the weight of all the sins of the people who would ever live on earth—even yours and mine. It was a great burden, and the pressure was so great that he bled from every pore. Heavenly Father sent an angel to comfort Jesus. We should be very grateful for what Jesus did for us.

Finally the suffering ended, and Jesus came out of the garden. But wicked men were waiting to take him away. The men took Jesus to their leaders, who said Jesus should die for saying he was the Son of God. But Jesus had been telling the truth. He had done nothing wrong, but the wicked men put him in prison and ordered him to be crucified.

Scripture:

And he was withdrawn from them . . . and kneeled down and prayed, and there appeared an angel unto him from heaven, strengthening him. And being in an agony he prayed more earnestly: and his sweat was as it were great drops of blood falling down to the ground.
(Luke 22:41-44)

Visual Aid:
GAPK #227
Jesus Praying in Gethsemane

Scripture:

And they took Jesus, and led him away. And he bearing his cross went forth into a place called the place of a skull, which is called in the Hebrew Golgotha: Where they crucified him, and two others with him, one on either side, and Jesus in the midst.
(John 19:16-18)

Visual Aid:
GAPK #230
The Crucifixion

On the day that Jesus was crucified, wicked Roman soldiers beat him with whips and made fun of him. They pushed a crown of thorns onto his head and made him bleed.

The soldiers took Jesus to a hill near Jerusalem. They laid him down and nailed his hands and feet to a wooden cross. Then they lifted the cross off the ground. This hurt Jesus very much, but he prayed and asked Heavenly Father to forgive the soldiers who had crucified him. The soldiers didn't realize he was the Savior.

Jesus suffered on the cross for many hours. Finally Jesus said, "Father, into thy hands I commend my spirit." Then Jesus died. There was a big earthquake and the sky went dark. Then the Roman soldiers looked at each other and felt bad. They were worried Jesus had told the truth. He truly was the Son of God.

Jesus visits the Spirit World

After Jesus died on the cross, his body was taken by one of his followers and put in a tomb. But the Savior was still alive as a spirit. Jesus was now very happy. He knew he had completed his mission on earth, and had become the Savior.

Jesus traveled to the Spirit World, where many wonderful people waited to greet him, such as Adam and Eve, Enoch, Noah and Abraham, and all the ancient prophets. The Savior told these righteous people to serve as missionaries in the Spirit World. They would teach the gospel to the other spirits who didn't know about Jesus.

When we die, we will also go to the Spirit World. We will be greeted there by our friends and relatives who died before us. We may even get to teach others about Jesus.

Scripture:

While this vast multitude waited and conversed, rejoicing in the hour of their deliverance from the chains of death, the Son of God appeared, declaring liberty to the captives who had been faithful; and there he preached to them the everlasting gospel. (D&C 138:18-19)

Visual Aids:
GAPK #231
The Burial of Jesus
GAPK #232
Jesus' Tomb

Chapter 10

Jesus is resurrected

Jesus appears at the Garden Tomb

Scripture:

Jesus saith unto her, Mary. She turned herself, and saith unto him, Rabboni; which is to say, Master. Jesus saith unto her, Touch me not; for I am not yet ascended to my Father; but go to my brethren, and say unto them, I ascend unto my Father.
(John 20:16-17)

Visual Aid:
GAPK #233
Mary and the Resurrected Lord

The body of Jesus had been buried in a tomb in a garden. On the third day after Jesus was crucified, two angels rolled away the stone in front of the tomb. On that morning a friend of the Savior, Mary Magdalene, came to visit the tomb. She was very sad to see the stone rolled away, and that the Savior's body was gone. Mary started crying.

Soon Mary realized someone was standing behind her. She thought it was the gardener. She asked him what he had done with the Savior's body. But then she heard Jesus say, "Mary."

She knew his voice, and she was suddenly very happy. Jesus was resurrected! His body and spirit had reunited in perfect form. Jesus told her to go tell the apostles that she had seen him, and that he would meet with them soon.

Jesus appears to the apostles

After Mary Magdalene had talked with Jesus near the Garden Tomb, she ran back to the house to tell the apostles. But when she told them she had seen Jesus, they didn't believe her.

Then Jesus appeared in the room. It seemed hard to believe, and the apostles were afraid. But Jesus told them, "Peace be unto you."

Jesus showed them the marks in his hands and in his feet, and they felt the Savior's wounds with their own hands. They knew for themselves that he was a resurrected man. They were no longer afraid. They were very happy. Jesus also appeared to many other people in the next forty days. He taught the apostles how to run the church. Then Jesus returned to heaven.

Scripture:

Jesus . . . stood in the midst, and saith unto them, Peace be unto you. And when he had so said, he showed unto them his hands and his side. Then were the disciples glad, when they saw the Lord. (John 20:19-20)

Visual Aid:
GAPK #234
Jesus Shows His Wounds

Jesus tells Peter to "Feed my sheep"

Just before Jesus was crucified, the apostle Peter was asked by three different people if he knew the Savior. Each time he told them no. After the third time, Peter felt bad, and he was sure Jesus would never forgive him. But Jesus knew that Peter was meant to be the leader of the Savior's church after Jesus returned to heaven.

After Jesus was resurrected, Peter and his friends became fishermen again. But one morning the Savior was waiting for them on the shore. He had cooked breakfast for them. Then he asked Peter, "Lovest thou me?" Peter said, "Yes, Lord."

Then Jesus said, "Feed my sheep," meaning "Watch over the church members." The Savior did this two more times to show Peter the importance of teaching the gospel. Jesus knew that Peter was now ready to be the leader of the church.

Scripture:

He saith unto him the third time, Simon, son of Jonas, lovest thou me? . . . And he said unto him, Lord, thou knowest all things; thou knowest that I love thee. Jesus saith unto him, Feed my sheep. (John 21:15-17)

Visual Aid:
GAPK # 229
Peter's Denial

Jesus visits the Nephites

When Jesus died, the people on the American continent felt many earthquakes. Many wicked people were killed. Plus, there was darkness for three days. This was very scary. People didn't know what was happening. Then they heard the Savior's voice coming from heaven. He told them he had been resurrected. The daylight returned, and the people gathered at the temple in the city of Bountiful. The Savior soon visited them there.

Jesus came down from the sky in a beautiful cloud of light. Then Jesus let everyone touch the marks in his hands and feet, and he taught them the gospel. He especially blessed the little children.

Jesus chose twelve men to lead his church among the Nephites, and they became a righteous people. For more than 200 years they followed the Savior's teachings and were very happy.

Scripture:

And it came to pass that the multitude went forth, and thrust their hands into his side, and did feel the prints of the nails in his hands and in his feet; and this they did do, going forth one by one until they had all gone forth, and did see with their eyes and did feel with their hands, and did know of a surety and did bear record, that it was he, of whom it was written by the prophets, that should come.
(3 Nephi 11:15)

Visual Aid:
GAPK #315
Christ Appears to the Nephites

Chapter 11

The Church of Jesus Christ is restored

The Apostasy covered the earth

Scripture:

Let no man deceive you by any means: for that day shall not come, except there come a falling away first, and that man of sin be revealed, the son of perdition.
(2 Thessalonians 2:3)

Visual Aid:
GAPK #235
Go Ye Therefore

Jesus told his apostles that his Second Coming wouldn't take place for many years. He told them the temple in Jerusalem would be destroyed, and all the apostles would be killed. The true church would be taken from the earth, and the priesthood power would be lost. In the Americas, the true church would also be lost. This would be called the Apostasy.

Jesus told the apostles there would be many wars and earthquakes before he came back in glory. Other churches would be formed, but they wouldn't have the true teachings or the true priesthood power. But the Savior knew his church would be restored in the latter days by Joseph Smith, and the church would become strong in the last days. We live in that time today.

The way is prepared to restore
The Church of Jesus Christ

The Savior had told his prophets that his church would be restored in the last days before his Second Coming. But the church would have to be formed in a land of freedom. So Jesus carefully planned how it would happen. First he inspired the Pilgrims and many other good people to cross the ocean and come to America.

Then he inspired many special men, such as George Washington, Benjamin Franklin and Thomas Jefferson, to seek for freedom. They fought the Revolutionary War and became a free people. They wrote the Constitution and formed the United States. Now the prophecies could be fulfilled. The Church of Jesus Christ could be restored and bless the earth's people.

Scripture:

And for this purpose have I established the Constitution of this land, by the hands of wise men whom I raised up unto this very purpose, and redeemed the land by the shedding of blood.
(D & C 101:80)

Visual Aid:
GAPK # 608
Christ and Children From
Around the World

63

Heavenly Father and Jesus visit Joseph Smith

Scripture:

When the light rested upon me I saw two Personages, whose brightness and glory defy all description, standing above me in the air. One of them spake unto me, calling me by name and said, pointing to the other — This is My Beloved Son, Hear Him! (Joseph Smith History 1: 17)

Visual Aid:
GAPK #403
The First Vision

A few years after the United States was formed, a young man named Joseph Smith was looking for the true church. He was confused because there were many churches, and they all claimed to be the true one.

Joseph knew there could only be one true church, so he decided to pray about it. He went to a grove of trees near his home and asked Heavenly Father which church he should join. To his surprise, Joseph was visited by Heavenly Father and his son Jesus Christ. They appeared above him surrounded by a bright light. They told Joseph not to join any of the churches.

Heavenly Father and Jesus told Joseph he had been chosen to restore The Church of Jesus Christ to the earth again.

Joseph Smith restores the Church

Joseph Smith was a very special prophet. He experienced many wonderful things. Jesus sent the angel Moroni to teach Joseph about the Gold Plates, which Joseph translated into the Book of Mormon. The Savior later sent other heavenly messengers to restore the power of the priesthood. Now the time was right for The Church of Jesus Christ to be on the earth again.

Jesus told Joseph to restore the church, which he did on April 6, 1830 at Peter Whitmer's farmhouse in Fayette, New York.

Jesus told Joseph what he wanted the church's name to be. The Savior said it should be called The Church of Jesus Christ of Latter-day Saints.

Scripture:

For thus shall my church be called in the last days, even The Church of Jesus Christ of Latter-day Saints.
(D&C 115:4)

Visual Aid:
GAPK #408
Melchizedek Priesthood
Restoration

Chapter 12

Jesus will come again

Scripture:

And then shall ye know that I have seen Jesus, and that he hath talked with me face to face, and that he told me in plain humility, even as a man tell the another in mine own language, concerning these things.
(Ether 12:39)

Visual Aid:
GAPK #520
Gordon B. Hinckley

Ever since the church was restored in 1830, the Savior has had a prophet on the earth. The Savior has also called twelve apostles in our day, just as he did when he lived in Jerusalem. These men are special witnesses of Jesus Christ, and they have the power to teach the gospel and do miracles through the priesthood.

The Savior gave many important revelations to Joseph Smith. Our prophet today is Gordon B. Hinckley, and Jesus continues to tell him many important things. The Savior has told his prophets that great events still await members of the church. The gospel will be preached in every nation. Also, the members of the church will build a beautiful city called New Jerusalem before the Savior's Second Coming. We can do our part to help the church grow by living righteously today and following the words of the prophet.

The Second Coming

Jesus has promised to come to earth again. He will come in the sky, with many angels at his side. The earth will be cleansed by fire, and those who have lived wickedly will be destroyed. Only good people and things will still be on earth. Then a thousand years of peace will begin.

Everyone on earth will know the Savior has come again, and he will rule over the whole earth. Jesus will visit Jerusalem and many other places where his followers are gathered.

At the Second Coming all the righteous people who have died will be resurrected. Each person's spirit and body will reunite and be made perfect. These resurrected people will visit with their family members and friends. This will be a wonderful time for the righteous.

Scripture:

For I will reveal myself from heaven with power and great glory, with all the hosts thereof, and dwell in righteousness with men on earth a thousand years, and the wicked shall not stand. (D&C 29: 11)

Visual Aid:
GAPK #238
The Second Coming

The Millennium

When Jesus comes again, the righteous people of the earth will be very happy to see him. This period of time will be called the Millennium and will last for 1,000 years. The earth will become a beautiful garden, like when the Garden of Eden was on the Earth. Animals will be nice to each other, and there will be peace everywhere. Jesus will be the king of the earth. He paid the price for our sins, and has made it possible for us to live with him forever.

Children that are born in the Millennium will grow up and obey all the commandments. It will be a wonderful time when temple work will be completed for all the righteous people who have lived on the earth. The Savior will be in charge of this great work.

Scripture:

And the earth shall be given unto them for an inheritance; and they shall multiply and wax strong, and their children shall grow up without sin unto salvation. For the Lord shall be in their midst, and his glory shall be upon them, and he will be their king and their lawgiver.
(D&C 45: 58-59)

Visual Aids:
GAPK #100
Creation- Living Creatures
GAPK #239
The Resurrected Jesus Christ

Life in the Celestial Kingdom

When the Millennium is over, the earth will be changed. It will become a celestial world, where the people who earned a place in the Celestial Kingdom will live.

There will be a final judgment, and those who have followed the Savior's teachings will be allowed to live as resurrected beings in celestial glory. This is called Eternal Life, and it is the greatest gift that Heavenly Father and Jesus can give us.

None of these wonderful blessings would be possible if Jesus hadn't completed the Atonement for us. He loves us very much and suffered great pain to pay the price for our sins. We should always be thankful to the Savior for what he has done for us, and show our love by following him.

Scripture:

These are they who are just men made perfect through Jesus the mediator of the new covenant, who wrought out this perfect atonement through the shedding of his own blood. These are they whose bodies are celestial, whose glory is that of the sun, even the glory of God, the highest of all.
(D&C 76:69-70)

Visual Aid:
GAPK #240
Jesus the Christ

71

About the authors

Watch for upcoming volumes in the Tiny Talks series!

Tammy and Chad Daybell live in Springville, Utah, with their five children.

Tammy Douglas Daybell was born in California and moved to Springville as a teenager. She served as Springville High's yearbook editor and played the drums in the marching band. She attended BYU as an advertising major. Her kids keep her pretty busy, but in her spare time she enjoys reading, gardening, and designing websites.

She is the illustrator for this volume.

Chad Daybell was born in Provo, Utah, and was raised in Springville. He served in the New Jersey Morristown Mission among the Spanish-speaking people.

In 1992 he graduated from BYU with a bachelor's degree in journalism, where he served as the City Editor of *The Daily Universe*. Later, he worked for several years as a newspaper editor at *The Standard-Examiner* in Ogden, Utah.

Chad has also written the award-winning LDS series ***The Emma Trilogy***.

The trilogy's novels—***An Errand for Emma***, ***Doug's Dilemma***, and ***Escape to Zion***—are exciting adventures written for teenagers and adults that teach the three missions of the church. Through the time-travel experiences of the Daltons, a modern-day LDS family, readers first step back into the past with Brigham Young, then later view the church's future in New Jerusalem.

Visit **www.cdaybell.com** to learn more about the authors and these LDS titles.